-Mapographica-

the
NATURAL
WORLD

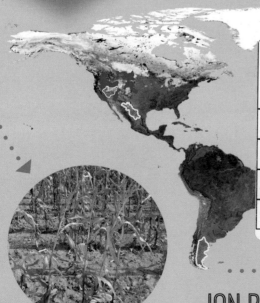

JON RICHARDS *and* ED SIMKINS

WAYLAND

CONTENTS

4–5 OUR PLANET

6–7 CLIMATE

8–9 BIODIVERSITY

10–11 FORESTS

12–13 DESERTS

14–15 ADAPTING FOR SURVIVAL

16–17 ANIMAL MIGRATION

18–19 ENDANGERED SPECIES

20–21 OCEANS

22–23 PLATES AND QUAKES

24–25 VOLCANOES

26–27 NATURAL DISASTERS

28–29 CLIMATE CHANGE

30–31 MAPPING THE WORLD, WEBSITES AND GLOSSARY

32 INDEX

ACKNOWLEDGEMENTS

First published in Great Britain in 2015 by Wayland
Copyright © Wayland, 2015
All rights reserved
Editor: Julia Adams
Produced for Wayland by Tall Tree Ltd
Designer: Ed Simkins
Editor: Jon Richards

Dewey number: 570.2'23-dc23
ISBN 978 0 7502 9154 5

Wayland, an imprint of
Hachette Children's Group
Part of Hodder and Stoughton
Carmelite House
50 Victoria Embankment
London EC4Y 0DZ

An Hachette UK Company

www.hachette.co.uk
www.hachettechildrens.co.uk

Printed and bound in Malaysia

10 9 8 7 6 5 4 3 2 1

Picture credits can be found on page 32

Our natural PLANET

Earth is an ever-changing planet. Deep beneath its crust, churning molten rock pushes and pulls on the surface, creating volcanoes and earthquakes and shaping the land. The planet is also home to a vast range of different ecosystems, from the dark ocean depths to lush rainforests and freezing polar ice sheets.

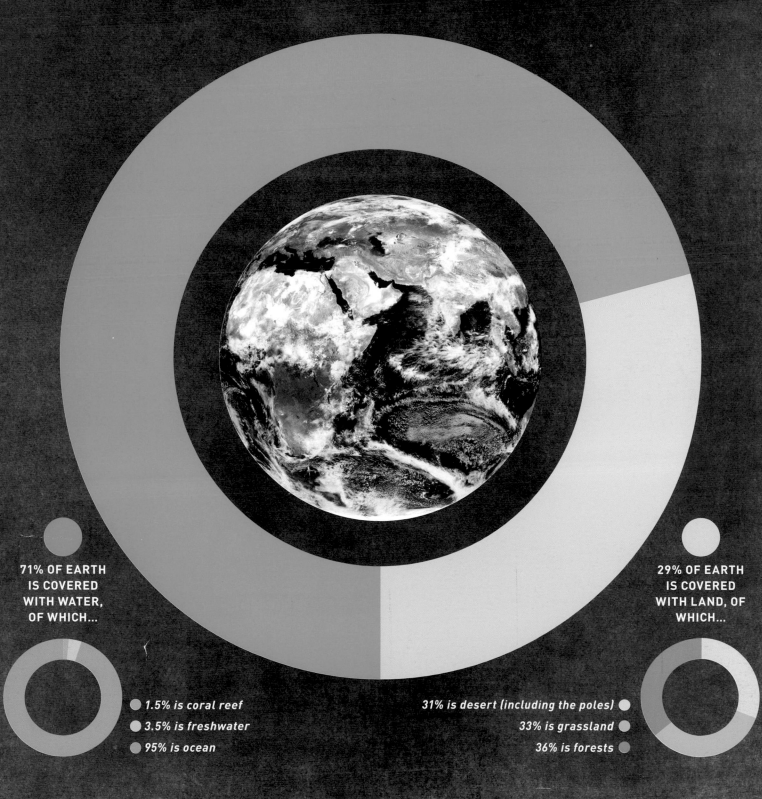

71% OF EARTH IS COVERED WITH WATER, OF WHICH...

29% OF EARTH IS COVERED WITH LAND, OF WHICH...

- 1.5% is coral reef
- 3.5% is freshwater
- 95% is ocean

- 31% is desert (including the poles)
- 33% is grassland
- 36% is forests

Our PLANET

The world is divided into large landmasses, called continents, and together these cover 148.94 million sq km, which is a little under 30 per cent of Earth's total surface area. The continents feature towering peaks that stretch high into the atmosphere, rivers that wind for thousands of kilometres and vast islands.

NORTH AMERICA

EUROPE

ASIA

AFRICA

SOUTH AMERICA

OCEANIA

NORTH AMERICA

Highest mountains

Denali
6,194 m

Mt Logan
5,959 m

Pico de Orizaba
5,636 m

Longest rivers

Missouri 3,767 km

Mississippi 3,734 km

Yukon 3,187 km

Largest islands

Greenland
2,166,086 km²

Baffin
507,451 km²

Ellesmere
196,235 km²

SOUTH AMERICA

Highest mountains

Aconcagua
6,995 m

Oyos del Salado
6,893 m

Pississ
6,793 m

Longest rivers

Amazon 6,437 km

Paraná 4,880 km

Madeira 3,250 km

Largest islands

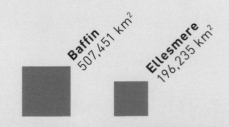

Isla Grande de
Tierra del Fuego
248,000 km²

Marajó
40,100 km²

Chiloé
8,394 km²

EUROPE

Highest mountains

Elbrus 5,642 m
Kazbek 5,033 m
Mont Blanc 4,810 m

Longest rivers

Volga 3,692 km

Danube 2,860 km

Ural 2,428 km

Largest islands

Great Britain 229,885 km²
Iceland 102,775 km²
Ireland 84,421 km²

AFRICA

Highest mountains

Kilimanjaro 5,895 m
Kenya 5,199 m
Mawenzi 5,149 m

Longest rivers

Nile 6,853 km

Congo 4,700 km

Niger 4,180 km

Largest islands

Madagascar 587,000 km²
Socotra 3,796 km²
Réunion 969 km²

ASIA

Highest mountains

Mt Everest 8,848 m
K2 8,611 m
Kanchenjunga 8,586 m

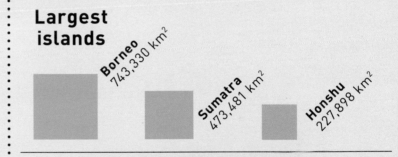

Longest rivers

Yangtze 6,300 km

Yellow 5,464 km

Lena 4,400 km

Largest islands

Borneo 743,330 km²
Sumatra 473,481 km²
Honshu 227,898 km²

OCEANIA

Highest mountains

Wilheim 4,509 m
Giluwe 4,367 m
Mauna-Kea 4,205 m

Longest rivers

Murray 2,375 km

Murrumbidgee 1,485 km

Darling 1,472 km

Largest islands

New Guinea 462,840 km²
New Zealand South island 151,215 km²
New Zealand North island 113,729 km²

CLIMATE

Types of climate vary greatly around the world, depending largely on a region's location between the Equator and the poles. They can be hot or cold, have huge differences in the amount of rain they get, and they can have different seasons, where conditions vary from one month to the next.

WORLD CLIMATE TYPES

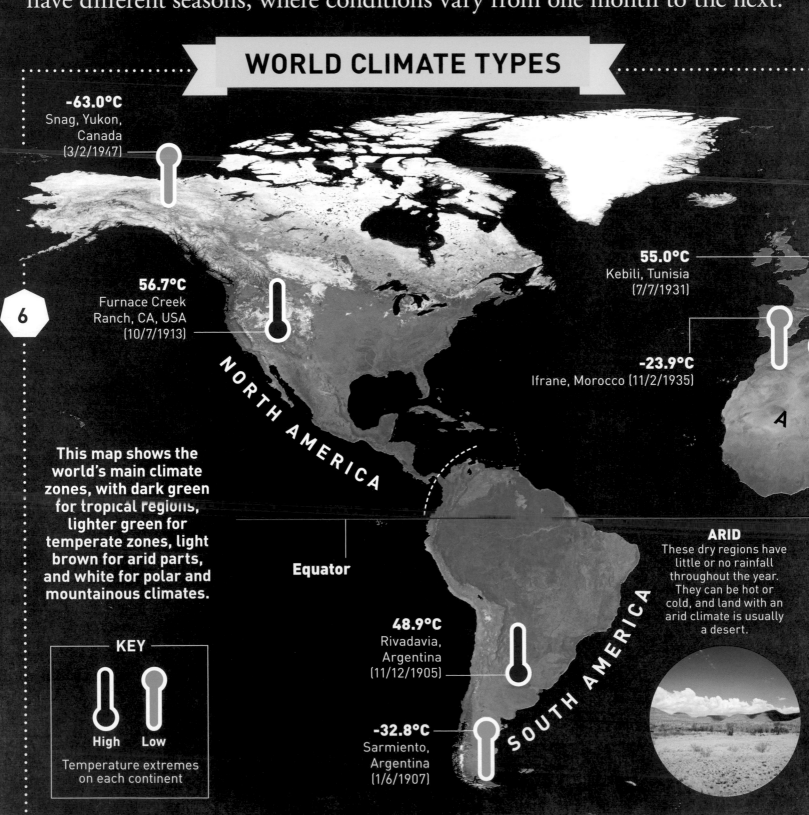

-63.0°C
Snag, Yukon, Canada (3/2/1947)

55.0°C
Kebili, Tunisia (7/7/1931)

56.7°C
Furnace Creek Ranch, CA, USA (10/7/1913)

-23.9°C
Ifrane, Morocco (11/2/1935)

NORTH AMERICA

A

This map shows the world's main climate zones, with dark green for tropical regions, lighter green for temperate zones, light brown for arid parts, and white for polar and mountainous climates.

Equator

ARID
These dry regions have little or no rainfall throughout the year. They can be hot or cold, and land with an arid climate is usually a desert.

48.9°C
Rivadavia, Argentina (11/12/1905)

SOUTH AMERICA

KEY

High   Low

Temperature extremes on each continent

-32.8°C
Sarmiento, Argentina (1/6/1907)

MEDITERRANEAN

Named after the climate around the Mediterranean Sea, this climate is found in other parts of the world, such as Chile, California, USA, and South Africa. It has warm, dry summers and cool, wet winters.

TEMPERATE

Temperate zones lie midway between the tropics and the poles. They usually have mild summers and winters and rainfall levels can be high throughout the year.

POLAR

The climates around the poles are cold throughout the year, but especially during the winter months when the Sun may not rise above the horizon. Close to the poles, sea and ground are covered by thick sheets of ice.

48.0°C
Athens, Greece
(10/7/1977)

-58.1°C
Ust 'Schugor,
Russia (21/12/1978)

-67.8°C
Verkoyansk and Oimekon, Russia
(5/2/1892, 7/2/1892, 6/2/1933)

EUROPE

ASIA

AFRICA

54.0°C
Tirat Tsvi, Israel
(21/6/1942)

7

MOUNTAINS

Highland regions, such as the Andes and the Himalayas, have no distinct seasons. Conditions vary the higher you climb.

OCEANIA

TROPICAL

Tropical regions lie on either side of the Equator. They can be tropical wet, with high levels of rainfall throughout the year, or tropical dry, with two distinct seasons – a wet season and a dry one.

50.7°C
Oodnadatta,
Australia
(2/1/1960)

-23.0°C
Charlotte Pass, NSW,
Australia (29/6/1994)

BIODIVERSITY

Some parts of the world, such as rainforests, are home to thousands of different types, or species, of living things, while others, such as the poles and hot deserts, may only have a handful.

BIODIVERSITY RANGE AND HOTSPOTS

This map shows the countries with the highest and lowest numbers of species. This variation of species is known as the region's biodiversity.

KEY

Top 5 | Bottom 5

Biodiversity
(total number of amphibian, bird, mammal, reptile and vascular plant species)

Biodiversity Hotspots
Biodiversity hotspots are areas that have at least 1,500 species of plants, but are under threat because they have lost more than 70 per cent of the original plant cover.

Haiti
5,716
species

Portugal
5,714
species

Spain
5,796
species

Mexico
28,836
species

Colombia
54,649
species

Brazil
59,851
species

NUMBER OF SPECIES IN THE WORLD

Thousands of new species are discovered every year, and estimates show that there are far more species that are yet to be found.

Animals
estimated
7.77 million
(953,434 already identified, which is only **12%**)

Protozoa
estimated
36,400
(8,118 already identified which is only **22%**)

Algae
estimated
27,500
(13,033 already identified which is only **47%**)

Plants
estimated
298,000
(215,644 already identified which is only **72%**)

Fungi
estimated
611,000
(43,271 already identified which is only **7%**)

TOTAL ESTIMATE **8.74 MILLION** SPECIES ON PLANET EARTH

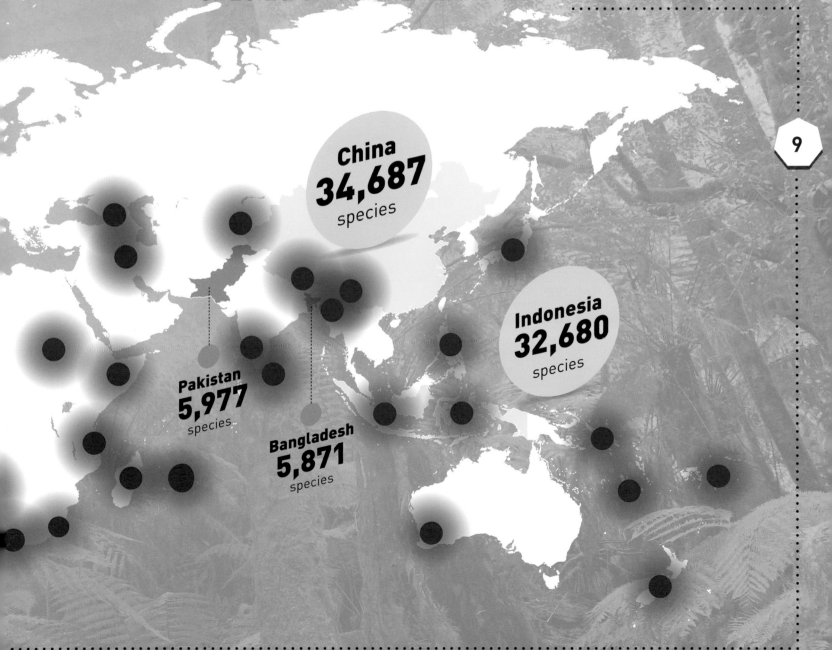

China
34,687
species

Indonesia
32,680
species

Pakistan
5,977
species

Bangladesh
5,871
species

FORESTS

The world's forests are not evenly distributed around the globe – two-thirds of them lie in just ten countries: Russia, Brazil, Canada, USA, China, Australia, Congo, Indonesia, Peru and India. However, these forests are under threat as trees are cut down for fuel or to make way for farms and towns.

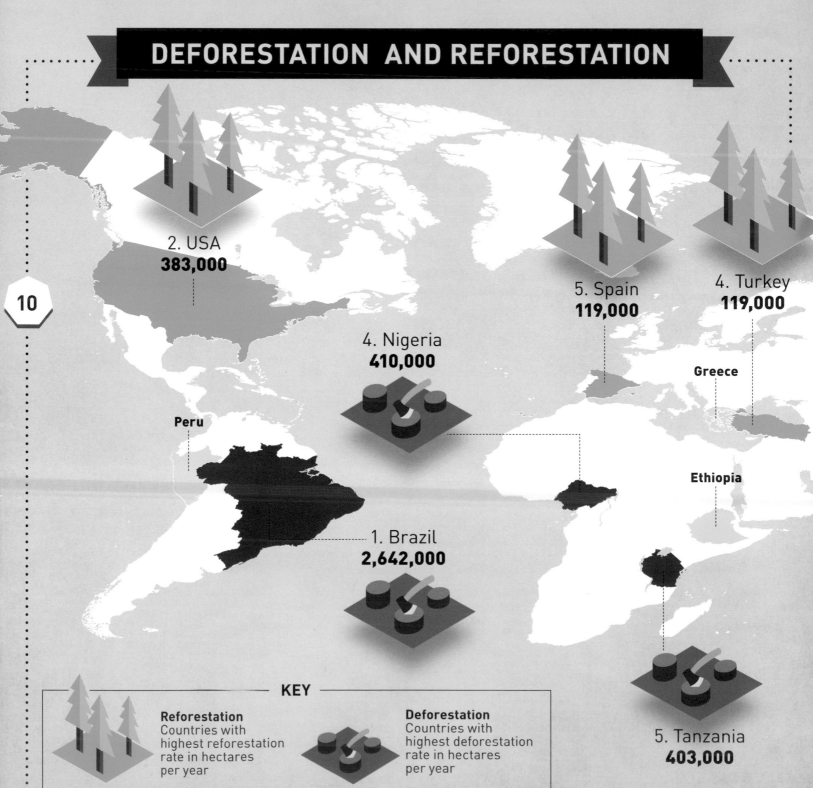

DEFORESTATION AND REFORESTATION

2. USA
383,000

5. Spain
119,000

4. Turkey
119,000

Greece

4. Nigeria
410,000

Peru

Ethiopia

1. Brazil
2,642,000

KEY

Reforestation
Countries with highest reforestation rate in hectares per year

Deforestation
Countries with highest deforestation rate in hectares per year

5. Tanzania
403,000

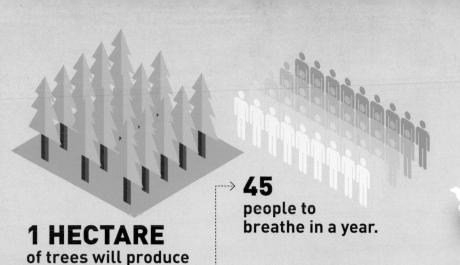

1 HECTARE
of trees will produce
enough oxygen for

45
people to
breathe in a year.

**THE AMAZONIAN
RAINFOREST** ALONE
PRODUCES ABOUT
20 PER CENT OF THE
WORLD'S OXYGEN.

Reforestation

The Bonn Challenge sees countries committing to
restoring 150 million hectares of forest by 2020 –
that's a bigger area than the whole of Peru.

20%

The biggest commitment
to reforestation is by
Ethiopia, which has
pledged to restore
22 million hectares
(more than 20 per cent
of its land area).

Global deforestation rate

In total, nearly
**13 million
hectares**
of forest are lost each year.
This is an area equivalent
to Greece.

11

1. China
2,986,000

3. Vietnam
207,000

3. Indonesia
498,000

2. Australia
562,000

Rare species

One of the rarest species in the world is the
Wollemi pine. It was thought to be extinct until
about 100 trees were discovered in a remote valley
near Sydney, Australia, 1994. The species is at
least 200 million years old.

DESERTS

A desert is a region that receives less than 25 centimetres of precipitation each year. Deserts cover about one-third of Earth's land area and they can be hot or cold. They are covered in sand, rocky scrub or ice sheets.

MAJOR DESERTS

12

GREAT DUNE OF PYLA, ARCACHON BAY
France
107m
Tallest sand dune in Europe

Great Basin
North America
490,000 km² ---- **7**

ISAOUANE-N-TIFERNINE SAND SEA
Algeria
430m
Tallest sand dunes in Africa

9

Chihuahuan
Mexico,
453,000 km²

KEY

⬡ **Major Deserts**
The world's major deserts and their sizes

Danger of desertification
These regions are usually found next to existing deserts and may become deserts themselves.

◯ **Tallest sand dunes**
Dunes are created when wind blows over large areas of sand, creating waves, or dunes, some of which can be hundreds of metres tall.

DUNA FEDERICO KIRBUS
Argentina
1,230m
Tallest sand dune in the world

Sahara
Africa
9,100,000 km²

5

Patagonian
South America,
670,000 km²

Singing Sand

'Singing Sand' can sometimes be heard in a desert when a surface layer of sand flows down a dune, perhaps disturbed by someone walking near the top. The noise can be a low boom or a shrill squeak with a volume of up to 105 decibels – as loud as a revving snowmobile engine.

Syrian
Arabian Peninsula
490,000 km²

Gobi
China and Mongolia
1,300,000 km²

(4)

(8)

13

BADAIN JARAN DUNES
China
500m
Tallest sand dunes in Asia

(2)

(3)

Arabian
Arabian Peninsula
2,600,000 km²

Great Victoria
Australia
647,000 km²

(6)

(7)

Kalahari
Africa
570,000 km²

Antarctic
Antarctica
14,200,000 km²

MOUNT TEMPEST, MORETON ISLAND
Australia
285m
Tallest coastal sand dune

(1)

Adapting for SURVIVAL

Around the world, different animals have evolved different characteristics to suit their environment and way of life. This can include thick fur to stay warm in the polar chill or a super-long neck to grasp food that's far out of the reach of others.

ANIMAL HABITATS

Polar bears

RANGE
ARCTIC
....

Polar bears have thick fur and a layer of fat to keep them warm in the freezing Arctic. They can also swim for many kilometres from one patch of sea ice to another in search of prey.

Saltwater crocodiles

RANGE
EASTERN INDIA, SOUTHEAST ASIA AND NORTHERN AUSTRALIA
....

These huge reptiles use their enormous size to ambush and overpower prey. They have powerful tails to push them through the water and their eyes and noses are on top of their heads so that they can remain submerged and out of sight of their unsuspecting prey.

Kangaroos

RANGE
AUSTRALIA
....

Kangaroos have long, powerful legs, which they use to bound across the large grasslands of Australia.

Gorillas

RANGE
AFRICA
....

Gorillas have thick fur to protect their skin from biting insects and to keep them warm. They have large teeth to help them chew the plants and leaves that make up their diet.

Camels

RANGE
AFRICA, MIDDLE EAST AND SOUTH ASIA
....

Camels have adapted to life in dry desert climates. They have long eyelashes to keep sand out of their eyes and they can close their nostrils to keep sand out of their noses. Their humps are full of fat and act as a food store, and they have huge feet so that they don't sink into the sand.

Giraffes

RANGE
AFRICA
....

Giraffes use their long necks to reach leaves high up in trees and out of reach of other animals' grasp. They are also able to spot far-away predators. They have strong hearts to push blood up to their heads.

Blue whale

RANGE
ALL OCEANS
....

The largest animal that has ever lived is able to grow to enormous size because its body weight is supported by water. Its mouth is filled with large frills called baleen plates, which the whale uses to filter out tiny creatures, called plankton, from the water to eat.

African elephant

RANGE
AFRICA
....

The largest land animal on the planet has huge ears, which it uses to control its body heat. Its long trunk is used to pick up food and objects, scoop up water, sniff things and to feel and communicate with other elephants.

Wandering albatross

RANGE
SOUTHERN OCEAN
....

Albatrosses have long, thin wings, which they use to catch ocean winds and glide for hours on end without even a single flap.

Octopus

RANGE
ALL OCEANS
....

This mollusc doesn't have an internal skeleton. This means that it can squeeze its body into tiny cracks to hide from predators or to search for prey.

15

Animal
MIGRATION

Many animals take part in regular journeys in search of food, water or to find somewhere to give birth and raise young. These migrations can cover thousands of kilometres or just a few hundred metres.

MAJOR MIGRATION ROUTES

This map shows some of the greatest migrations undertaken by different animals over land and sea, and through the air.

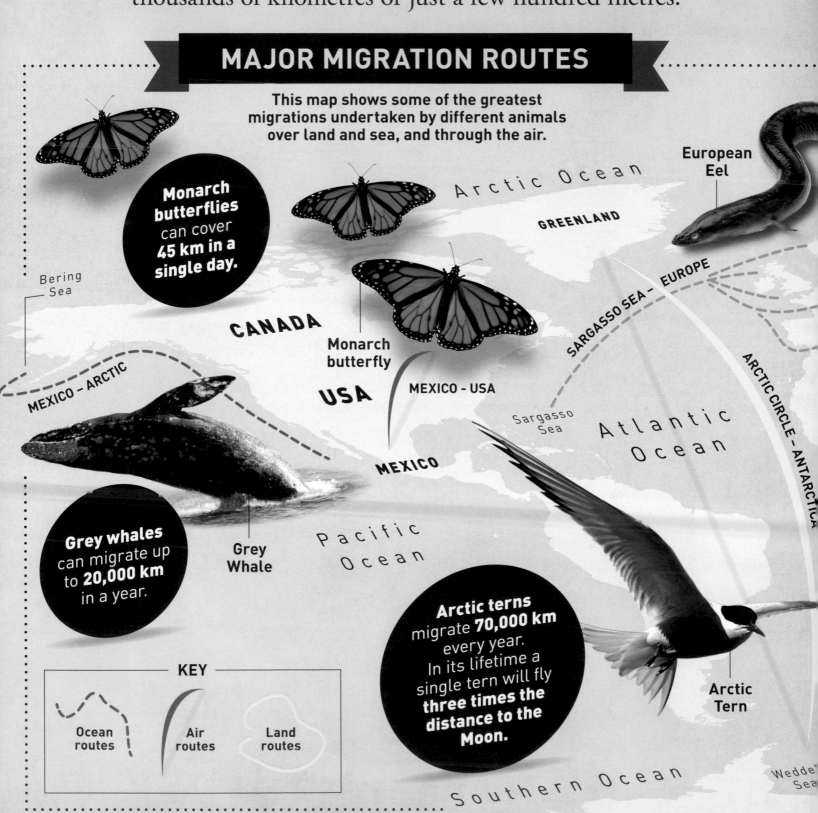

Monarch butterflies can cover **45 km in a single day.**

Bering Sea

Arctic Ocean

GREENLAND

European Eel

CANADA

Monarch butterfly

SARGASSO SEA – EUROPE

MEXICO – ARCTIC

USA

MEXICO – USA

Sargasso Sea

Atlantic Ocean

ARCTIC CIRCLE – ANTARCTICA

MEXICO

Grey whales can migrate up to **20,000 km** in a year.

Grey Whale

Pacific Ocean

Arctic terns migrate **70,000 km** every year. In its lifetime a single tern will fly **three times the distance to the Moon.**

Arctic Tern

KEY

Ocean routes

Air routes

Land routes

Southern Ocean

Weddell Sea

ZOOPLANKTON

Every day, huge numbers of tiny animals called zooplankton (right), travel hundreds of metres up and down the ocean in search of food, in a movement called vertical migration.

Wandering glider dragonflies migrate by using fast-moving winds that blow **at altitudes of nearly 6.5 km.**

A single leatherback turtle swam more than **20,500 km from Indonesia to America** in 2003.

A European eel will migrate to breed and lay up to **10 million eggs at once.**

Wandering glider dragonfly

Leatherback Turtle

Wildebeest

INDIA

INDIA - AFRICA

Indian Ocean

INDONESIA

CHRISTMAS ISLAND

AUSTRALIA

KENYA

TANZANIA

Nearly **1.5 million wildebeest** take part in the **largest land migration on the planet.**

Red crab

On Christmas Island near Indonesia, nearly **50 million red crabs** migrate to the sea at the same time to lay eggs.

A N T A R C T I C A

Endangered
SPECIES

Scientists believe that more than 20,000 species of plants and animals are on the brink of extinction. This includes about one-third of all amphibian species, a quarter of the world's mammals and an eighth of all bird species.

THREATENED SPECIES

This world map shows how many species of plant and animal are under threat in a selection of countries from around the planet.

CANADA

USA
1,203

UK

FRANCE

MEXICO
959

NIGER

CENTRAL
AFRICAN REP.

SENEGAL

18

UNDER THREAT

In general, those countries that have a great range of biodiversity, such as those that contain rainforests, have the highest number of species under threat. The country with the highest number of threatened species is Ecuador.

48
are molluscs

26
are reptiles

43
are mammals

93
are birds

171
are amphibians

Ecuador has
2,282
ENDANGERED
SPECIES,
of which...

1,837
are plants

CAMEROON
632

14
are invertebrates

50
are fish

BRAZIL
1,008

ARGENTINA

WHY DO SPECIES BECOME ENDANGERED?

There are many reasons why plant and animal species become endangered. Some species are worth a lot of money and are collected or hunted, while other species are threatened by pollution and disease. Perhaps the greatest threats come from habitat loss, climate change and the appearance of foreign species.

Habitat loss
Habitat destruction, such as the clearing of forests for mines or cities, reduces the area a species can live in, as well as its food supply.

Climate change
A change in a region's climate can destroy a habitat and reduce the amount of food sources, making it difficult for a species to survive.

Invasive species
A new, foreign species may compete for the same food as a native species, or it can even feed on the native species, reducing its numbers.

KEY
Number of threatened species
(plants and animals) in selected countries:

High
500 species and above

Medium
between 100–500 species

Low
fewer than 100 species

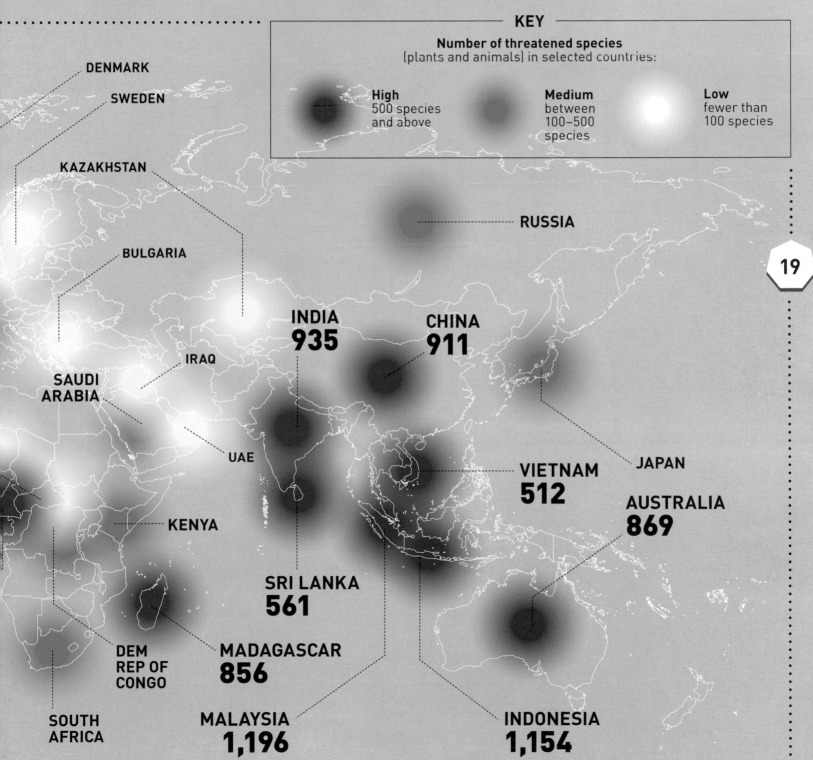

DENMARK

SWEDEN

KAZAKHSTAN

RUSSIA

BULGARIA

IRAQ

SAUDI ARABIA

INDIA
935

CHINA
911

UAE

JAPAN

VIETNAM
512

AUSTRALIA
869

KENYA

SRI LANKA
561

DEM REP OF CONGO

MADAGASCAR
856

SOUTH AFRICA

MALAYSIA
1,196

INDONESIA
1,154

OCEANS

Earth's oceans are vast, and we have only explored less than 5 per cent of them. Beneath the surface are thousands of undiscovered species, as well as physical features such as volcanoes, canyons and mountain ridges.

THE WORLD'S OCEANS

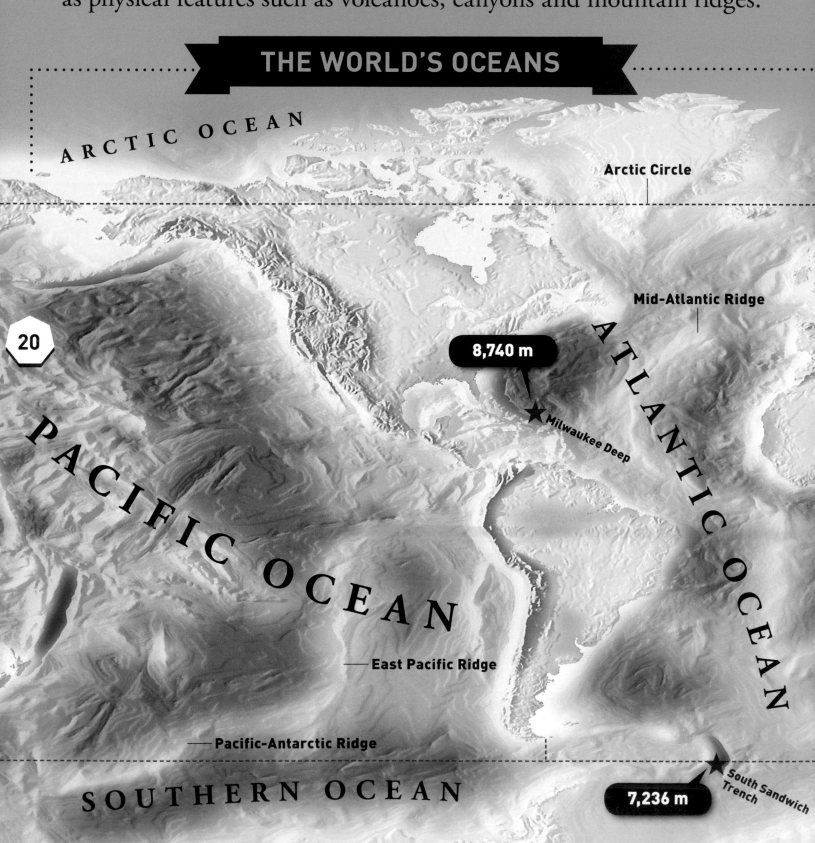

ARCTIC OCEAN

Arctic Circle

Mid-Atlantic Ridge

8,740 m

★ Milwaukee Deep

ATLANTIC OCEAN

PACIFIC OCEAN

East Pacific Ridge

Pacific–Antarctic Ridge

SOUTHERN OCEAN

7,236 m

★ South Sandwich Trench

ANTARCTICA

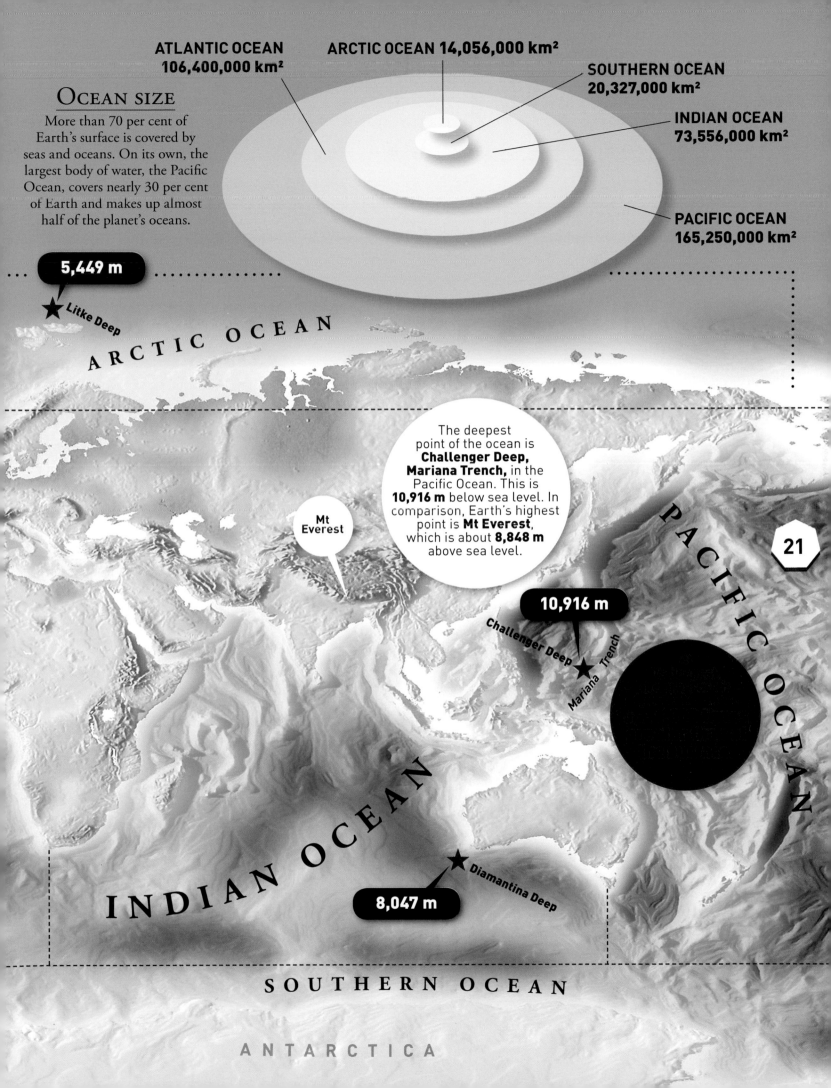

ATLANTIC OCEAN 106,400,000 km²

ARCTIC OCEAN 14,056,000 km²

SOUTHERN OCEAN 20,327,000 km²

INDIAN OCEAN 73,556,000 km²

PACIFIC OCEAN 165,250,000 km²

Ocean Size

More than 70 per cent of Earth's surface is covered by seas and oceans. On its own, the largest body of water, the Pacific Ocean, covers nearly 30 per cent of Earth and makes up almost half of the planet's oceans.

5,449 m

Litke Deep

ARCTIC OCEAN

The deepest point of the ocean is **Challenger Deep, Mariana Trench,** in the Pacific Ocean. This is **10,916 m** below sea level. In comparison, Earth's highest point is **Mt Everest**, which is about **8,848 m** above sea level.

Mt Everest

PACIFIC OCEAN

10,916 m

Challenger Deep

Mariana Trench

INDIAN OCEAN

8,047 m

Diamantina Deep

SOUTHERN OCEAN

ANTARCTICA

Plates and QUAKES

Earth's crust is split up into huge blocks, called tectonic plates. These move about slowly, crashing into each other, scraping together or pulling apart, triggering powerful earthquakes with devastating effects.

TECTONIC PLATES

This map shows the world's tectonic plates, the direction in which they are moving and the locations of the most powerful and deadliest earthquakes.

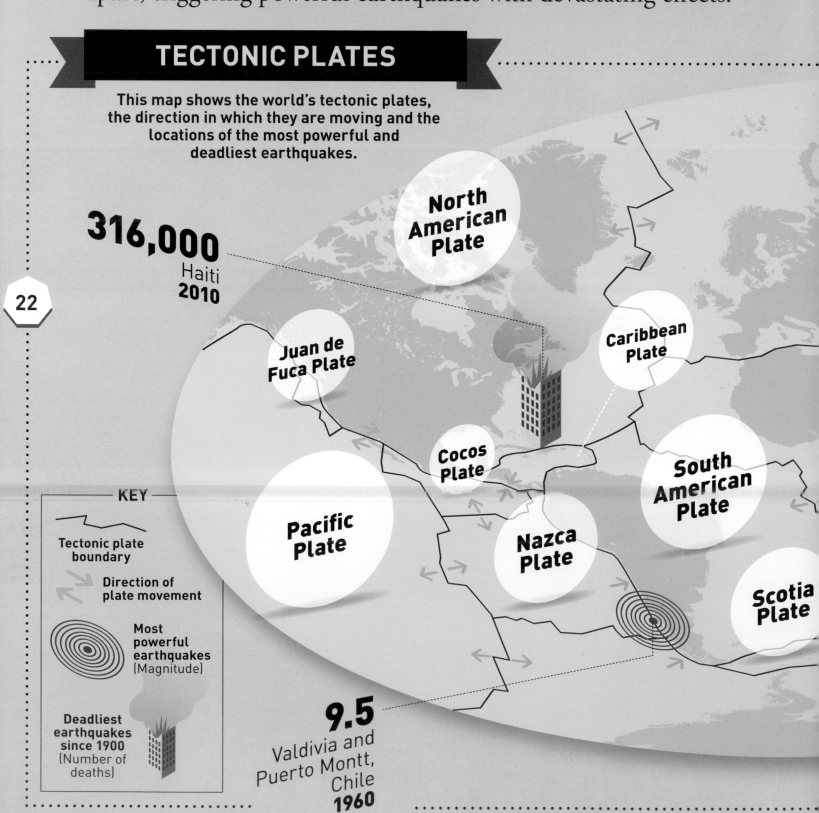

316,000
Haiti
2010

North American Plate

Caribbean Plate

Juan de Fuca Plate

Cocos Plate

South American Plate

Pacific Plate

Nazca Plate

Scotia Plate

9.5
Valdivia and Puerto Montt, Chile
1960

KEY

Tectonic plate boundary

Direction of plate movement

Most powerful earthquakes (Magnitude)

Deadliest earthquakes since 1900 (Number of deaths)

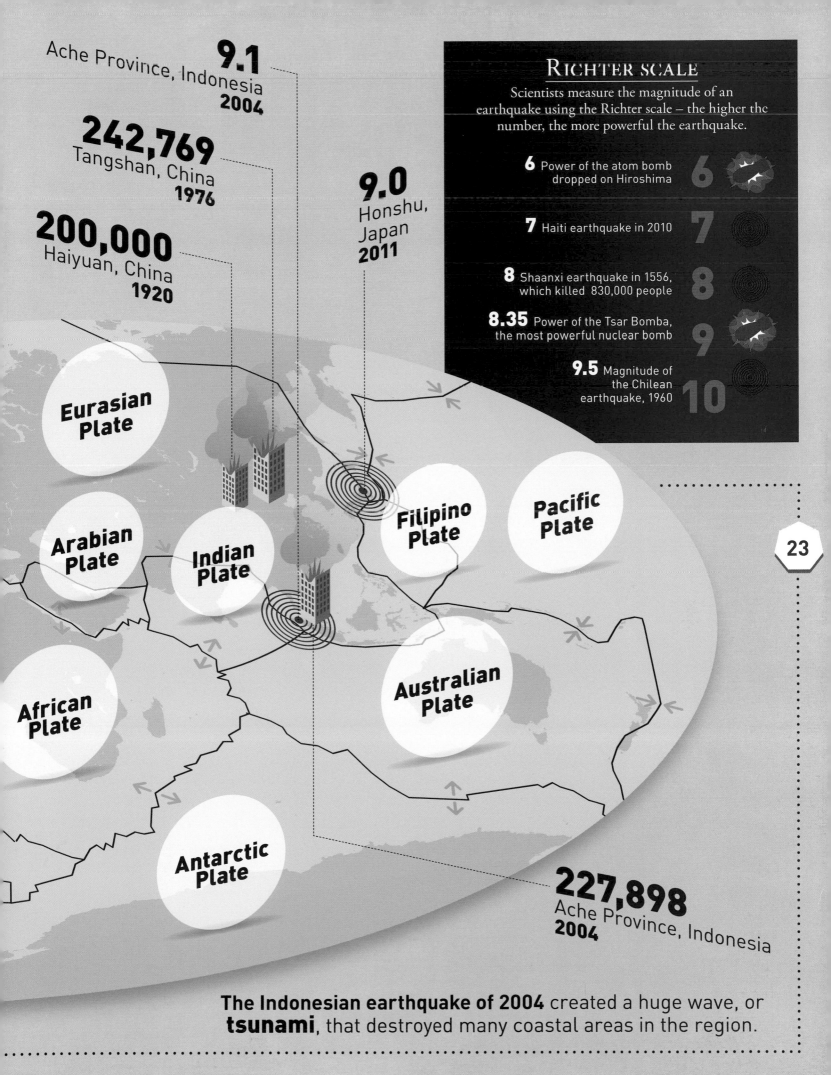

Ache Province, Indonesia **9.1** **2004**

242,769
Tangshan, China
1976

200,000
Haiyuan, China
1920

9.0
Honshu,
Japan
2011

Eurasian
Plate

Arabian
Plate

Indian
Plate

Filipino
Plate

Pacific
Plate

African
Plate

Australian
Plate

Antarctic
Plate

227,898
Ache Province, Indonesia
2004

The Indonesian earthquake of 2004 created a huge wave, or
tsunami, that destroyed many coastal areas in the region.

VOLCANOES

Volcanoes are holes in the Earth's crust through which super-hot molten rock, or lava, pours out of the ground. Most of them are found around the edges of Earth's tectonic plates, but some are found in the middle of a plate, where the rock is thin enough for lava to erupt.

ACTIVE VOLCANOES

MEDITERRANEAN
Movement between the Eurasian plate and the African plate causes cracks or fractures through which molten rock wells up, creating volcanoes throughout southern Europe.

Siberia

Ring

Kilimanjaro

Indonesia

EAST AFRICA
The eastern edge of the African plate is splitting, creating a huge crack, or rift. Kilimanjaro is a dormant volcano in this region and is the tallest mountain in Africa.

INDONESIA
Movement between the Australian and Eurasian plates has created a string of volcanoes along the southern edge of Indonesia.

KEY

Areas of volcanic activity

DIFFERENT TYPES OF VOLCANO

Caldera
A large crater or bowl that is formed when land collapses during an eruption.

Shield
Formed by runny lava, which hardens to create a large volcano with a low profile.

Dome
Formed by thick lava, which hardens to create a circular mound.

Composite
Also known as a stratovolcano, this is formed by layers of lava, rock and ash that build up over successive eruptions.

of Fire

YELLOWSTONE
Beneath the Yellowstone National Park is one of the biggest volcanoes on the planet. This supervolcano last erupted more than 600,000 years ago.

ALASKA
Tectonic activity in the northern Pacific has created a string of volcanoes that stretch from Alaska to Siberia.

Yellowstone Park

EASTERN PACIFIC
The ring of volcanoes around the Pacific Ocean is known as the Pacific Ring of Fire. The eastern edge of this ring is created by movement between the Pacific, Filipino and North American plates.

HAWAII
The Hawaiian volcanoes are found in the middle of the Pacific Plate, far away from any plate boundaries. Here, the plate is so thin that it creates a hotspot where volcanoes are formed.

There are more than

1,500

active volcanoes around the world. An active volcano is one that has erupted in the last 10,000 years.

New Zealand

ANDES
The volcanoes of the Andes are formed by the Nazca Plate being pushed beneath the South American Plate as the two crash into each other.

Natural
DISASTERS

Regular seasonal extremes of rainfall and temperature create severe storms that lash regions and cause huge amounts of damage. Other deadly disasters include avalanches and huge earthquake-created tsunamis.

THE WORST DISASTERS

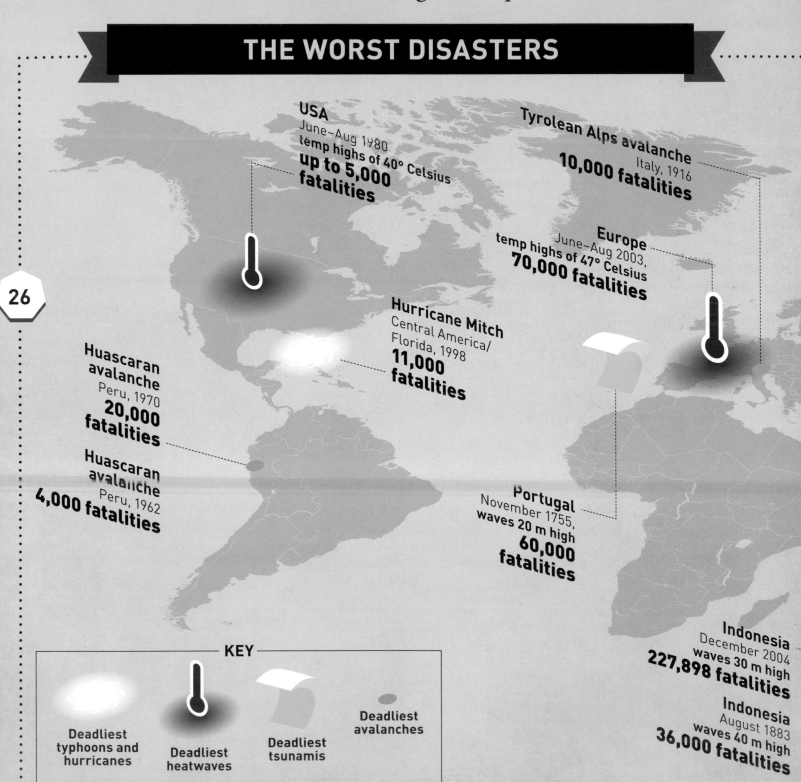

USA
June–Aug 1980
temp highs of 40° Celsius
up to 5,000 fatalities

Tyrolean Alps avalanche
Italy, 1916
10,000 fatalities

Europe
June–Aug 2003,
temp highs of 47° Celsius
70,000 fatalities

Hurricane Mitch
Central America/
Florida, 1998
11,000 fatalities

Huascaran avalanche
Peru, 1970
20,000 fatalities

Huascaran avalanche
Peru, 1962
4,000 fatalities

Portugal
November 1755,
waves 20 m high
60,000 fatalities

Indonesia
December 2004
waves 30 m high
227,898 fatalities

Indonesia
August 1883
waves 40 m high
36,000 fatalities

KEY

Deadliest typhoons and hurricanes

Deadliest heatwaves

Deadliest tsunamis

Deadliest avalanches

DEADLY EVENTS

As well as the four events shown here, natural disasters can include earthquakes and volcanic eruptions, floods, blizzards, droughts, tornadoes, wildfires and even meteorite impacts.

Typhoons and Hurricanes
Massive swirling storms called cyclones, typhoons or hurricanes can measure hundreds of kilometres across.

Avalanches
Huge slides of snow that crash down mountain slopes are known as avalanches. They can travel at speeds of up to 400 km/h.

Heatwaves
Prolonged periods of high temperatures are called heatwaves. They can trigger fires and can be dangerous to vulnerable people, such as the elderly and very young.

Tsunamis
These are enormous waves that are usually triggered by earthquakes and underwater volcanic eruptions. These waves rush ashore and destroy everything in their path, before sweeping back out to sea.

Russia
July–Sept 2010
temp highs of 44° Celsius
56,000 fatalities

India
May–June 2003,
temp highs of 35° Celsius
1,500 fatalities

Bhola Cyclone
Bangladesh, 1970
500,000 fatalities

Bangladesh Cyclone
Bangladesh, 1991
138,366 fatalities

Japan
July–Sept 2010
temp highs of 35° Celsius
1,718 fatalities

Super Typhoon Nina
China, 1975
229,000 fatalities

Cyclone Nargis
Myanmar, 2008
138,366 fatalities

Japan September 1498
waves estimated 10–20 m
31,000 fatalities

Japan
March 2011
waves 10 m high
18,000 fatalities

Climate
CHANGE

Throughout its history, Earth's temperatures have varied, creating ice ages and warmer periods. Scientists believe that temperatures could increase by as much as 6°C over the next century, and this could have dramatic effects.

RISING SEA LEVELS

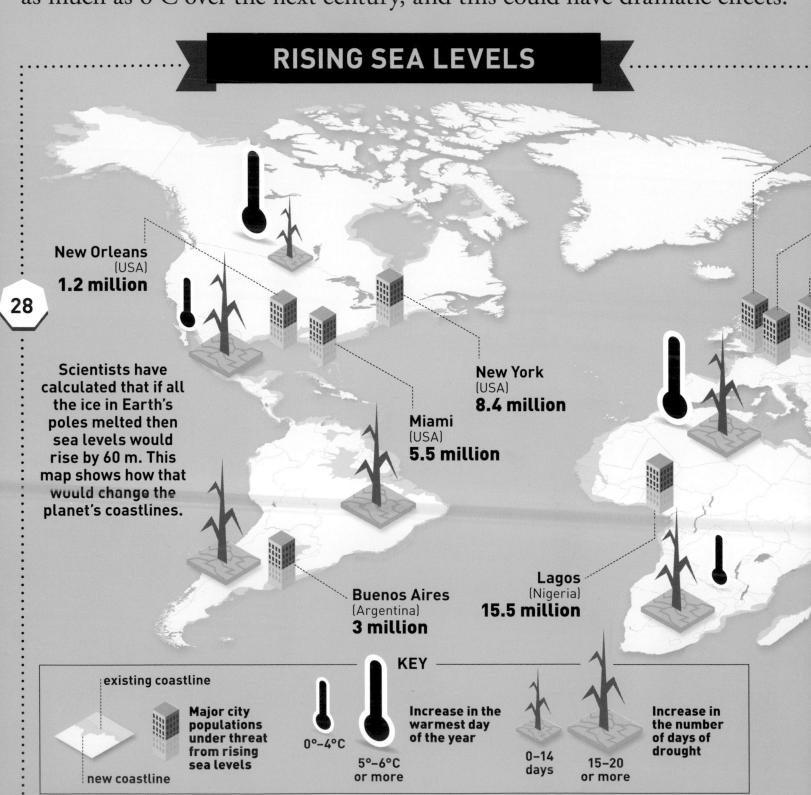

New Orleans
(USA)
1.2 million

Scientists have calculated that if all the ice in Earth's poles melted then sea levels would rise by 60 m. This map shows how that would change the planet's coastlines.

New York
(USA)
8.4 million

Miami
(USA)
5.5 million

Buenos Aires
(Argentina)
3 million

Lagos
(Nigeria)
15.5 million

KEY

existing coastline

new coastline

Major city populations under threat from rising sea levels

0°–4°C

5°–6°C or more

Increase in the warmest day of the year

0–14 days

15–20 or more

Increase in the number of days of drought

COSTS TO MAJOR CITIES IF SEA LEVELS RISE

Miami (USA) US$3.5 trillion
Guangzhou (China) US$3.4 trillion
New York (USA) US$2.1 trillion
Kolkata (India) US$2 trillion
Shanghai (China) US$1.8 trillion

London (UK)
8.6 million

Amsterdam (Netherlands)
1.6 million

Copenhagen (Denmark)
1.9 million

Kolkata (India)
11.8 million

Dhaka
(Bangladesh)
17.5 million

Shanghai
(China)
23.9 million

Mumbai
(India)
21 million

Tokyo
(Japan)
37.8 million

Guangzhou
(China)
10.3 million

Hong Kong
(China)
7.2 million

Ho Chi Minh City
(Vietnam)
9.2 million

DROUGHT

A drought is when a region experiences below-average rainfall for an extended period of time. Droughts can cause crops to fail, leading to famine. The worst famine in history occurred in 1876–1879 in northern China when there was little rainfall for three years, leading to between 9–13 million deaths.

Mapping the WORLD

The maps in this book are two-dimensional representations of our ball-shaped world. Maps allow us to display a huge range of information, including the size of the countries and where people live.

PROJECTIONS

Converting the three-dimensional world into a two-dimensional map can produce different views, called projections. These projections can show different areas of the Earth.

GLOBE
Earth is shaped like a ball, with the landmasses wrapped around it.

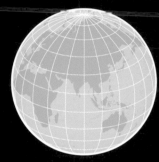

CURVED
Some maps show parts of the world as they would appear on this ball.

FLAT
Maps of the whole world show the landmasses laid out flat. The maps in this book use projections like this.

TYPES OF MAP

Different types of map can show different types of information. Physical maps show physical features, such as mountains and rivers, while political maps show countries and cities. Schematic maps show specific types of information, such as routes on an underground train network, and they may not necessarily show things in exactly the right place.

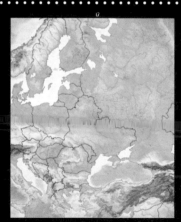

Physical map

Political map

Schematic map

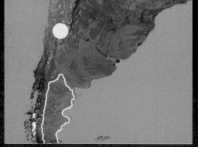

Coloured regions

Scaled symbols

MAP SYMBOLS

Maps use lots of symbols to show information, such as blue lines for rivers and colours for different regions. Some of the symbols in this book show the locations of subjects, or the symbols are different sizes to represent different values – the bigger the symbol, the greater the value.

GLOSSARY

BIODIVERSITY
The number and range of different plant and animal species that live in a region.

CLIMATE
The long-term weather conditions that a region experiences. Climate can be affected by how close a region is to the Equator, physical features such as mountains and how close it is to the ocean.

CONTINENT
One of seven large land masses that make up Earth's land surface.

DEFORESTATION
The clearing of large areas of forest, usually to make way for farms, mines or urban areas.

DESERTIFICATION
When regions become deserts.

DORMANT VOLCANO
A type of volcano that has not erupted for a long period of time, but could still erupt in the future.

DROUGHT
An extended period when very little rain falls.

ENDANGERED
When the numbers of a species have become so low, that it is in danger of becoming extinct.

LAVA
Molten rock that has reached Earth's surface during a volcanic eruption.

MIGRATION
The movement of animals to a new area, usually in search of food, water, partners to mate with, or a suitable place to raise young.

REFORESTATION
The planting of new forests to replace those that have been cut down.

RICHTER SCALE
The scale used to measure the strength of an earthquake – the higher the number, the more powerful the tremor.

SPECIES
A group of living organisms that are very similar to each other and can reproduce with each other to produce fertile offspring.

TECTONIC PLATES
The large pieces of Earth's surface that fit together to form the crust. These pieces are crashing into each other, pulling apart or rubbing against one another.

TEMPERATE
Used to describe a region that is midway between the Equator and the poles. Temperate regions have mild weather conditions.

TROPICAL
Used to describe a region that lies on either side of the Equator. Tropical regions have warm weather conditions.

TSUNAMI
A large wave caused by an underwater earthquake or volcanic eruption.

31

WEBSITES

WWW.NATIONALGEOGRAPHIC.COM/KIDS-WORLD-ATLAS/MAPS.HTML
The map section of the National Geographic website where readers can create their own maps and study maps covering different topics.

WWW.MAPSOFWORLD.COM/KIDS/
Website with a comprehensive collection of maps covering a wide range of themes that are aimed at students and available to download and print out.

HTTPS://WWW.CIA.GOV/LIBRARY/PUBLICATIONS/THE-WORLD-FACTBOOK/
The information resource for the Central Intelligence Agency (CIA), this offers detailed facts and figures on a range of topics, such as population and transport, about every single country in the world.

WWW.KIDS-WORLD-TRAVEL-GUIDE.COM
Website with facts and travel tips about a host of countries from around the world.

INDEX

A

African elephant 15
arctic tern 15
arid climate 6
avalanches 26, 27

B, C

biodiversity 8–9
blue whale 15
camels 15
climate 6–7
climate change 19, 28–29
coral reefs 3

D, E, F

deforestation 10, 11
desertification 12
deserts 3, 4, 8, 12, 13
droughts 27, 28, 29
earthquakes 3, 22, 23, 24, 27
European eel 16
extinction 18
forests 3, 10–11
fungi 9

G, H

giraffes 15
gorillas 15

grasslands 3
grey whale 16
habitat loss 19
Hawaii 25
heatwaves 26, 27
hurricanes 27

I, K, L

ice sheets 3
islands 4, 5
kangaroos 15
Kilimanjaro 24
lava 24
leatherback turtle 17

M

Mariana Trench 21
Mediterranean climate 7
migration 16–17
monarch butterfly 16
mountains 4, 5, 7, 20

O, P

oceans 3, 20–21
octopus 15
plants 9
polar bears 15
polar climate 7
protozoa 9

R

rainfall 6, 7, 26, 29
rainforests 3, 8, 11
red crab 17
reforestation 10, 11
Richter scale 23
rivers 4, 5

S

saltwater crocodiles 15
sand dunes 12, 13
seasons 6, 7
'singing sand' 13
species 8, 9, 18, 19, 20

T, V, W, Z

tectonic plates 22, 23, 24
temperate climate 7
tropical climate 7
tsunami 23, 24, 26, 27
volcanoes 3, 20, 24–25, 27
wandering albatross 15
wandering glider dragonfly 17
wildebeest 17
Wollemi pine 11
Yellowstone 25
zooplankton 17

The publisher would like to thank the following for their kind permission to reproduce their photographs:
Key: (t) top; (c) centre; (b) bottom; (l) left; (r) right
cover t, 1t, 4–5 all istockphoto.com/photokey, cover, 1c courtesy of NASA, cover bl, 1bl, 29l istockphoto.com/vesilvio, 3c courtesy of NASA, 6–7, 12–13, 24–25 courtesy of NASA, 6br istockphoto.com/Mlenny, 7tl istockphoto.com/ah_fotobox, 7tc istockphoto.com/Daniel Barnes, 7tr istockphoto.com/lopurice, 7cr istockphoto.com/wcjohnston,7bl istockphoto.com/KeithBinns, 8–9 background istockphoto.com/Keilchihiki, 11cr istockphoto/com/mikdam, 13tr istockphoto.com/Lucyna Koch, 14bl, 15tl istockphoto.com/Josef Friedhuber,14tc, 15tr istockphoto.com/MogensTrolle, 14tr, 15clt istockphoto.com/John Carnemolia,14ct, 15cl

istockphoto.com/yoglimogli, 14ctr, 15br istockphoto..com/aurigadesign, 14c, 15cr istockphoto.com/ultrapro, 14cr, 15crt istockphoto.com/Guenter Guni, 14cr, 15crb istockphoto.com/WLDavies, 14bc, 15clb courtesy of NOAA, 14br, 15bl istockphoto/com/hfrankWI,16tl istockphoto.com/groveb, 16cr istockphoto.com/doescher, 16br istockphoto.com/Gannet77, 16–17c dreamstime.com/Pipa100, 17t shutterstock.com/aquapix, 17ct shutterstock.com/Vishnevskiy Vasily,17cl istockphoto.com/bbuong, 17cr istockphoto.com/irin717, 17cb istockphoto.com, 19tl istockphoto.com/luoman, 19tc istockphoto.com/kikkerdirk, 19tr istockphoto.com/GordonImages, 27tl istockphoto.com/Harvepino, 27tr istockphoto.com/robh, 27ct istockphoto.com/RafalBelzowski, 27cr istockphoto.com/jdavidlong, 29t istockphoto.com/compassandcamera, 30c istockphoto.com/nicoolay, 30cr istockphoto.com/Manakin

GET THE PICTURE

Welcome to the world of visual learning! Icons, pictograms and infographics present information in a new and appealing way.

PLANET EARTH
9780750278461

SPACE
9780750278454

COUNTRIES
9780750285069

MACHINES AND VEHICLES
9780750281287

THE HUMAN BODY
9780750278685

NATURAL RESOURCES
9780750285205

THE HUMAN WORLD
9780750289856

ANIMAL KINGDOM
9780750285199

SPORT
9780750285229

THE NATURAL WORLD
9780750289863

ART AND ENTERTAINMENT
9780750285212

TECHNOLOGY
9780750285076

RECORD-BREAKING HUMANS
9780750297745

RECORD-BREAKING ANIMALS
9780750297653

RECORD-BREAKING BUILDINGS
9780750287470

RECORD-BREAKING EARTH & SPACE
9780750297738